# Liefie

First Edition

## Joseph Leo Hickey

Rev. L

Cover illustrations by Michael Thompson with images from Pixabay.

Some of these poems have appeared in the Instagram account @solisortus88.

Melodium House

www.MelodiumHouse.com
joseph@melodiumhouse.com

# *Introductory Information*

This book contains a story about a fictional biracial couple from fictional iterations of The United States and South Africa.

Harmonie, a South African political activist was murdered on December 24th, 2019. The murder was motivated by race and political opposition.

A few months later, her husband, Liefie was found dead in the United States, in Chicago. The investigation is pending but is presumed by many that the murder was motivated entirely by race.

Both died for no reason.

Racism is absurd.

These poems are their words.

Key:

*Harmonie*, Liefie, **Both**

"We [the EFF] are not calling for the slaughter of white people, at least for now."
-Julius Malema

"With a kiss I die."
-Romeo & Juliet

"I have overcome the world."
-Jesus Christ

# CD #1

**last night i had a dream**
we were escaping from volcanic eruptions
lava seeping through dirt
eternal questions
all of them were answered by the fire
i woke up without you
i couldn't find you
dreams sometimes seem very real
and i think about how people
on the other side of the ocean
have no way to express their thoughts
or to escape from regimes that want
to control them
and here they divide us into left
and right
or based on race
i am not any color,
i am American and regardless of who takes our home
this is where i live,
this is the place i love
you cannot take it from me
i've never felt so peaceful
it's just the thought of you
you came into my life and changed it
you fell down and set the motion in place
there is now something to write about
you were happy just to be in my arms
i've been trying to imagine worlds
in which magic is real
in which there is no uncertainty
in which i can feel what you feel
how you feel it
in which there is adventure
and something worth living our lives for
always anxiety about writing
hesitant to speak
something holding me back

that i don't understand
all i write about is everything i feel
i can never write about anything that isn't real
nothing is tangible unless i can hold it in my hands
because when i touch you
i know there is connection and not ambiguity
there is relief in knowing we made an imprint in time
together
the dream last night
people losing their homes to fire
questions about mortality
how can anything be worth it
if it ends at all,
i have music inside my heart

you have a memory
of being alone in the night
but the cadence of love brings us together
nothing in our lives seems to go as we planned
i want to explore the entire world with you
i want you to be here
my skin touching yours feels natural
you fall down and i follow you
you get up to kiss me
the summer evening i remember the warmth on my face
i have scars covered by light
and when the sun sets there will be darkness
you are next to me dreaming about leaving and
traveling the world
and i can imagine being anywhere with you
the first summer we spent together
and the morning after the rain
i want to hold you so close that you will feel me as a ghost
when i'm gone,
devotion
the moment when i realize memories and flashbacks in our
minds
are a form of time travel
we can feel what we felt years ago

i want to feel more
i want to experience everything but death
you will stare at a blank page for hours
until you begin to write
i am yours if you want me to be yours
we are only alive for a little while
the dreams i had about high school
i don't know where any of my classes are
and i can't find you
keep me close
there is music in my mind
i remember listening to songs about
how everything is possible
how within the universe there are no limits
it's how i feel with you
i sit down to write and the words flow freely

and i cannot stop writing about
how closed off our minds are
to those who are in need of help

i think you are full of what song is full of
i think you are full of what my youth is
invigorated, ready to surprise the world with a new melody
the lives we will live as we sing and dance together
i was walking beside the ocean
thinking about you
i hadn't met you yet but now you are here
you make me feel like i am falling through the clouds
forever

and tidal waves appear in the distance
and we cannot run from them,
i reach for your hand but nothing is there

and the water submerged me
in the name of the Father
and of the Son
and of the Holy Spirit

yesterday i was baptized
and chrismated
today i am dreaming of tidal waves
and the way i have no control
in which i run but there is no safe place

the next day
it is 6:19 pm and i'm about to go outside

i hold my love close to me as we walk together
and we see the lake,
she's in love with the beautiful world
she makes me feel secure
she makes me feel home
as the small waves approach the
the shore of the lake
i know i'll find her in my dreams
and the waves will swallow us

-Liefie

second death confirmed in Pretoria.
remember that we are here forever,
we build walls,
we wave guns,
we lie on the concrete and never get up again
Liefie, remember that we are here forever,

we drive down these streets together
and realize that we can forget our past mistakes,
and learn to hold each other,
and with you i feel calm,
as if my heart was overcome by
joy and exaltation,
peace and reconciliation,

i remember going outside
and sitting on the hill,
looking at the stars

i remember experiencing joy
when i realized
that love is tangible

and i never felt the way you make me feel before

i hear your voice
i ask God for the right words

but all voices fade into the desert of time

the truth is that all people will
regret the way they treated each other,
if we realized we all shared the same soul,
we would all hold each other and never let go,
instead of holding guns to each other's heads

the knife of betrayal

*the blood of disbelief*
*dripping down every side,*
*before we fall*

*we make the most of the life we've been given,*
*Liefie, thank you for being here*

*the day we forget about the truth in our own eyes*
*the moment when dreams and memories*
*are all that remains*
*when i am sure i will never see home again,*
*when the streets are filled with violence*
*when they kill me just because of the colour of my skin*
*when silence breaks through each morning*
*but it is not the silence of peace,*
*it is the silence of death, despair and anguish.*
*the days when we live under the yoke of oppression,*
*the days when the gun is pressed firmly against the*
*back of our necks*
*i am still in love with my Liefie*
*i am still drowning in the ocean of his love,*

*sometimes i feel music*
*sometimes i can feel the sunrise*
*and the nature of what it is*
*passing through symbol*
*reaching into reality*
*remember us when we are dead*
         *that we did nothing wrong*
*not responsible for anything our ancestors did*

*we need to feel invigorated by a new spirit*
*we need to have our lives changed*
*the years have passed*
*2011 seems so long ago*

*i am glad that we have today*
*i am glad that i can be here for you*
*even when i have no job*

*i will be here for you*
*when everyone else betrays you*

*when life becomes hell*
*when i become insecure about everything*

*melody and the force behind it*
*the summer and the days that pass*
*when we will never have a chance to repeat what happened before*

*we do not feel enough*
*we never end up where we want to be*

*there's always someone with the power to take everything i have*

*remember to live,*
*we are walking together through the dark*
*struggling to find our footing*

*the process of grieving,*
*we all wait our turn*
*we all are lost, it doesn't matter*
*which road we take*

*i am praying for forgiveness for everything i have done wrong*
*i am moving to the beat of a love song*
*i will never be found*
*i will be ecstatic when everyone else is mourning*

*waiting for the day when the light comes to*
*my front door*
*and floods the city and the slums,*
*flooding every avenue*
*showing that what we really need is*
*to survive and we know*
*that our time here                    feels like forever*

*i stood on the mountain where i told you my secrets*

the dawn covered my face,
almost as if the morning would wash away
my doubts and fears of the previous day

we had no chance
of living normal lives,
of not having someone take revenge on us
for crimes we had nothing to do with
we are in the wrong country

come closer to me, Liefie

remember the trip we took to the beach
when the sunlight covered your face
and i could see every crevice
clearly in the illumination
pure, truth, a vision of heaven
that we will forget
because there is violence in the world

if only i could hold you forever
and therefore never feel the anxiety of
not knowing what action to commit to
or not knowing anything about the future,

in the future i know we'll be together

there is magic in the air,
threatening to cast us into
a world where we will never feel
the sunlight again,

what we see is only superficial,
i only love what's underneath your skin

when the days pass
without you here,
the sunlight will disappear from my face
and no one will see inside my soul

*whenever i write a story about being away from*
*here,*
*i'm thinking about you,*
*because we could be anywhere in the world*
*together*
*and we would be happy*
*together*
*i see the look on your face when you're content*
*because despite the agony that each day brings,*
*you make me move to the beat of a love song*
*and through the chaos of the approaching storm*
*i know you will be here when it passes,*

*protests in the streets,*
*while i'm waiting for the new day*

*throwing rocks through the windows*
*i'm hoping for miracles,*

*gunshots in the distance*
*and i start weeping,*
*i'm praying for my world to change,*

*i want to go away somewhere*
*they will never find me*
*but then my voice would not be heard*

*i must stay so*
*people will hear me*

-Harmonie

the birds
that sing,
as the days passed, i would spend them recording each
moment
painting portraits of the world

surprised by what i see in the portraits

i put down my brush and never paint again

old wounds heal
as i explore the world
i will travel coast to coast
memories of Harmonie
songs she used to sing
fade away with the wind
take me far away from where i am comfortable

i walk the streets alone
i grab hold of a train and ride on it
to the next city
as the city lights flash in front of me

now there are no words to portray

the beauty, enormity, depth and viciousness of the world

it is the morning after the storm

and i spent last night in the homeless shelter,
and this morning i had to leave

 i walk till i see mountains
and i stand on top of one
and fall asleep and dream
that i am on top of a mountain
but Harmonie is here with me

scribbles on the pages of a notebook i haven't had the
strength to write in

i stay inside and hear the thunder and the rain

i run outside by the lake

and remember when we ran together

always intertwined like a song we will never forget

you were the song, i was the soul

like gravity i fell headfirst into you
skydiving and i could not escape from you

the gentle music of the rain pattering on the window
interrupted by thunder

i know each moment will disappear

i will never go back to South Africa

i dream of you but you are intangible
i fall into an ocean totally separate from everything
which we had before

we were so peaceful
lying in bed staring into your eyes
my hands on your face

all i can remember are gunshots

all i can feel is the mournful last moments of the memory
i wish i never had
life ends like a flash of lightning
all i need is a mechanism
a tool to express what i need and time

and i will create beautiful art
and we will all forget the colors of our skin

i miss the mournful breeze
i miss the beautiful and silent animals that used
to live here but now are gone
the storm destroyed their home

the silent and beautiful forest

*4*

spiritual death
running through the streets of their city
for the rest of my life

in another life we are legends
an example for all of history

"i wish i could be with you forever"

"i cry when i think about losing you"

we are never together when we use our differences as a
wedge between us

we are all human

we are only alive for a little while

i see you somewhere in your past
in a vision of your mind's eye

all songs are about love

i believe our love will save the world

*"kill the Boer*
*shoot the farmers*
*shoot them because of the colour of their skin"*

*murder rate climbs*
*police drop the ball*

*this has become*
*the place i hate the most*

*but in my past*
*i was safe*

*used to be my home*
*now unrecognizable*
*there used to be lovely flowers*
*there used to be beautiful trees*
*used to be charity between us when we were kids*

*if only i could figure out*
*what to do before i die*
*to help those in need*
*but i am tempted to pack up and leave*
*and never come back*
*mentally or physically*
*to not be chained*

*"slit their throats*
*kill the children*
*in front of their mothers"*

*if all i hear every day are threats of violence*
*if all we are is nothing but*
*unspeakable actions*
*then i will be your light*
*to lead you out of the darkness*
*take my hand*

*and no longer despair*

*this is my home*
*this is where i live*
*you cannot take it from me*
*i am not black or white*
*i am South African*
*i am someone you will find*
*going from each city*
*standing in the worst part of Durbs*
*when no one else wants to be there*
*when there is a firefight in the streets*
*when the police do not reach us in time*
*i am watching*
*but not helping*
*i am dying with you*

*when they take all our things from us*
*in our hotel room,*
*remember that there is nothing that can be taken from me*
*i have lost it all*
*because the years have passed more quickly than i ever*
*could imagine*

6

for deliverance from all affliction
and wrath
let us pray to the Lord
Lord have mercy

you are almost invisible to me
as if one day you were here
but now you are gone
my fear was always one day
this would happen

i recorded every moment we were together
but either way the memory faded

i wrote the words down in journals
everything you said
but the words are disappearing from the page

i kept collections of CDs we used to listen to
every night i used to record one and send it to you
you would listen to them because they helped you sleep

i am addicted to the sound of music
to the sound of melody
like you were addicted to my voice
you fell asleep listening to me
words i spoke
stories i wrote about far off
distant lands
where there is fulfillment
and something worth risking our lives for
you read stories on the news
about tragedies that happened in your country
and it made you cry

there are so many things to experience in the world
so many ways to run from death
but with no money and nothing i will walk the streets alone
but the one thing i wanted to say
i love you more than you will ever know
more than i will ever realize
more than words could ever show

7

*i read the bible and look for answers*
*but those words are disappearing too*
*as i read them, the words flutter and fly away*
*they never stay in my mind*
*as if they were never solid or tangible*
*i've always wanted you to know*
*even if you were never real*

*i am in love with every part of you*
*because you're the only thing i feel*

*8*

as one universe fades away
all that's left is pure
incorruptible and indestructible
the reality we all know
we aren't pretending at all

you were never gunned down in the street
you never held my hand
you          never looked into my eyes
and said          you were never leaving me

i will fill these pages with words that fill me with strength
words i want to share with the world

there is fire burning underneath my skin
burning it up inside
telling me that we will outlast the storm together
Jesus calmed the storm
with just a single word
i will resurrect you with a thousand words
that paint pictures of the world the way it could have been
the world we pushed away but have not lost forever
now is the time to wake up
one day i was walking New York streets
and then i was alone in Pretoria
i realize there are no guiding forces to take us by the hand
to lead us far away
where we are not falling into the hurricane
to take us on a long trek
to never return home
because we have fallen out of love with our home
we could forget everyone who ever lived

*we could forget our parents*

*we could forget our friends*
*we could become so close to the days when nothing is happening*
*the days when we don't have a job*
*to the days when we are living in the slums with nowhere to go*
*and nothing to do*
*because no one is listening, and no one is there*
*i read the bible again*
*but the words are not the same*
*they've changed and say something different*
*as if reality itself was changing*
*and there is no reference point*
*nothing solid to hold onto that is not subject to change*
*even the Word of God is not solid or unchangeable*
*if God is not here to save us, then who will lift us up*
*if you have left my life, then where will i find love?*

everyone in the world has one book inside of them,
all of their experiences that they need to tell

but not everyone has two books inside of them
i have a thousand books inside of me
a million pages
if you can hear the words i am saying
you should spread them to others
and we will change reality
we will change the way the world spins

end every ounce of racism, degree of true hatred,
end the wars that are pointless, the silence we spend alone
together we will build something beautiful

plain words that incarnate themselves into music,
whenever they are heard
that have the same exact effect
that make you want to move
that make you want to cry
that make you want to laugh
that make you never want to die

*but our enemy is time*
*as governments conspire against us*
*to take away our home*
*i know we will never feel fulfilment*
*we will always feel alone*
*i have ten thousand books inside me*
*ten million thoughts to say*
*each a dissertation*
*each a critical essay*
*proving why we need to change*
*that we are all human*
*we are not any colour*
*we are one together*
*because we all will bleed*
*and if you ever need someone beside you*
*you can always call on me*
*i will never leave you or retract anything i say*
*it might take forever but the first day of forever begins now*


*we have all of eternity*
*to fix this*

*9*

*there is a moment when*
*we realize the importance of every breath*
*we fall into the arms of death*

*and never realize anything again*

*all the people around do not have time*
*to help those with nothing*

*a broken piece of mirror*

*a gun ready to fire*

*if we saw ourselves we would take the bullets*

*out of the gun*

*and walk away*

*travel the world and think about our own place in it*

*all images of the world are gone*

*they all fade deeply into each other*

*and all of the colours mesh together*

*what i need is a way to distinguish one day*
*from the other*

*what i need is you to promise me*
*that i will not be alone*

*the moonlight illuminates the city*

*fills the crevices of my heart*

*10*

when i think of the cosmos

stars galaxies

vast expanses

where there is no life

i wonder
why we dream about the places
we will never reach
like a shooting star i crash and burn
reaching
for a spiritual truth beyond who i am
like space its expanse

you too are a mystery
i will not understand

i am happy when i am alone with
my thoughts

days
nights
dreams nightmares

we wake up and weather terrible storms
our homes become flooded
we forget the truth
in our own hearts
we forget the moonlight
illuminating it
from the night
when we first met
believe in what is brighter
than all created order
libraries of knowledge
are nothing

the passing days alone
are nothing
the days when we are together are
what is full of life

the air becomes easier to breathe
when we are fully alive

my heart has absorbed the truth from yours

i use it as a golden compass

that points me back to you

i am sitting in a library
listening to Owl City

writing these words
really i could be anywhere
i could be anyone
i could be climbing
scaling a mountainside

when i reach the top i am ecstatic
i could be running for miles
and when i reach the end
i take in
a thousand deep breaths
and afterwards fall asleep
but tomorrow
i will be kissing you

tomorrow i will be at peace
peace beyond all understanding

a calm like the wind when we are just married
and sleeping in a room on the beach

the sun is setting and the breeze fills us both with joy

*II*

seeing the world
through the light of the new day

                    everything is vibrant
                    everything is beautiful
and clear

the light changes everything

i will dream about the Owl City concert last night

i will dream about you in my arms
and how i cannot write
another word in a poem without thinking of you

isn't it remarkable how fast each day has passed?

now i'm not here with you
and     i can't remember much about the concert
except how happy i was

you vanished like melody
it is not always with us
but when it is there is peace
and reconciliation
when it is gone, we not only miss
its presence but also dream about it
and it is actually always with us
in some sense
because we are living the experience
that we heard about in the songs


inevitable
glorious
tragic

all of these words describe the music we listened to
together

clear
solid
warm
present

when i think about the future
i know that we will
spend either the rest of our lives together
or dreaming and yearning for the rest
of our lives for what we can never have

## 12

*in the*
*dusk of our lives*

*i sit on a swing bench*
*and wait for you to come out of the house*

*as we watch the setting of the sun*
*overlooking the lake*

*so many warm colours*

*so many brilliant waves of light*

*so many nights i will lay asleep*
*and feel totally content*
*as our hearts beat a million times together*

*you can never be certain of anything*
*you can never know for sure*
*that you are alive*
*and not dreaming*
*because my days with you were like*
*a vivid dream*
*and i could wake up at any second*

## 13

it grieves me to hear that you are suffering
it is the worst feeling i have ever felt

when you are stranded and alone
and i can't reach out to you

when you are paralyzed by what surrounds you
feelings welling up inside
and swell with sorrow

i am 8000 miles away from you
i am paralyzed
because you are in distress

*14*

the next day i heard from you
and learned that you had been rescued
from the worst night of your life

i flew down to see you
i held you close and didn't let go
you begged me never to leave you again
the simplicity
of a broken heart
the depth of
what the world used to be
but what we can never have again

*15*

*there are so many beautiful colours in the world*
*there is so much here to feel*
*there is so much to experience*
*and to laugh about*
*and so much we won't regret when we enter our old age*

*this is how we became so close*
*you are here, tangible*
*and you keep me from falling*
*i am here*
*you feel me too*
*you save me from drowning*
*you go to the highest heights because you wanted*
*to see the depth of the beautiful world*
*and to fall in love with it*
*i was drowning in the depths*
*of books and routine*

of each single and dreary day
you took me up and saved me
you fell and set the motions in place
when i reach for your hand you take it
you make me feel like only simple language could describe
because nothing would describe you specifically

we go and explore the world

we see the mountains, the trees,
the silent and beautiful plains
the silent and beautiful glaciers
the silent and beautiful morning
the looming and inevitable sunset
the dusk of the new day inevitably waking us
the mania of every silent hour
passing without telling us why
the violence that awaits us one day
but which we don't want to think about
visions of the future
will never come true

16

the moment
when panic sets into my mind
the moment when fear is all that controls my breathing
the next moment
when the knife is thrust into me
the seconds
when i am lying on the cold
ground
a few breaths
and then i am no longer breathing

*17*

you remember being in my room
and taking the books off the walls
i remember the notes you wrote me
i've kept them all

*18*

you are dead
so i pack up
and leave,
doesn't matter where i go

*19*

*i've made CDs of all the*
*voice notes you sent me*
*of songs you used to sing*
*i listen to them and i fall asleep*

*i wrote a book of poetry*
*and sent it to everyone i know*

*it's amazing how so few words*
*can change a life*

*20*

*love is inseparable from our being*
*because whenever i write*
*the only thing that motivates me is love*

*21*

going to sleep
and dream
about the trains
that are passing by

near my bed

going to wake up
and look at the sky
and hear the insects
and walk into the trees
feeling each branch against
my dark skin
going to forget
that you are not alive
when i see the beautiful things
that you were showing me

## 22

i am 22 years old tomorrow

i have lived enough to see
the world is both vicious and enchanting

## 23

one day in april
i had my home broken into
and everything dear to me stolen

one day in may
i reached out for your hand
and you pulled me
three times out of the water

one day in june
i saw you standing in the light
of the sun
on the shore where i was baptized

one day in july
we took a trip to the beach
and felt inebriated in each other's presence

one day in august you said
you wanted to marry me
and we were married at the end of the month

one day in september
i was walking surrounded by sunlight
with beautiful things
your hand in mine

one day in october
the world started to turn darker
and i was terrified
of what i saw on the news

one day in november
you disappeared
and had to flee far away from me

one day in december
i will always remember
that you lost your life
fighting for a better future

one day in january
the cold did not subside

one day in march i walked the world alone
and left never to find myself

*24*

*the truth is*
*i will never let go of you*
*the truth is*
*i will never leave you*

*25a*

i feel the light on my face warming it up
every moment of my life
we go on long runs together
and fall in love with the feeling we get
when we can't run anymore
when we know we are growing stronger

*25b*

*passion burning inside of us,*
*i'm in the back seat of a car*
*watching the farmlands disappear, the veld become a distant memory*
*watching the city come up over the horizon*
*and then i am watching the ocean crawl toward me*
*and then i am sleeping*
*and then i am dreaming*

*the warmth of this morning,*
*when i pull back the curtains*
*and inhale the light*

*i put on a U2 record*
*i live like death is inevitable*
*i am so tired during the night*
*i am filled with a magical force*
*i am filled with life and movement*
*and power*

*25c*

i am on a flight to South Africa,
        the world is the world

*26a*

*the new year has come,*
*i feel like life could go on for eternity*

*26b*

the trend is to forget what's right

*27*

i have always wanted
to learn how
to give inspiration to another soul

*28a*

*you feel the love*
*in every fibre of your being*

*28b*

there may be no solution
there may never be peace again

*28c*

there may be peace in the future
there may be ineffable joy

*28d*

*the air of fall is*
*a feeling*

*the air of fall is*
*memory*

*the air of fall is*
*the book i wanted to write*
*but never put pen to paper*

*the air of fall is the love and truth*
*i lost forever*

*the air of fall is the passing time of my youth*

*the air of fall is the book i started*
*reading but never finished because it made*
*me feel sad about myself and my own life*
*because even in the world of darkness*
*there is someone to grasp onto*

*you are my freedom*
*you are the one whose name i shout in the rain*
*you are the one whose name i shout in the snow*
*you are the one who has lost hope*
*you contain the spark of eternal glory*
*and become that spark and the match yourself*

*the days are still passing,*
*the nights still drag on for uncountable hours*

*Liefie, you remind me of my entire life*
*and how the hope i need,*
*i found it all with you*

*29*

on the train
hitching a ride to the next
city
where i will wander the streets
dreaming about what it would be like
to live a normal life

*30a*

*tomorrow i will wake up*
*and think you are here*
*but you aren't*

*30b*

grief comes when you cannot express your thoughts
in that same morning

*31*

*all of our experiences in life are repeating*
*a never-ending cycle*
*of need and searching*

we stop our car at the robots
and i kiss you every time

*32*

i will say all of the things you were thinking

but never brought yourself to say

i will be outside of your social circles

i will be walking the street, dressed all in black
as if the rest of my life was one long funeral
one long day filled with regret but not despair
because
no one can take my hope from me

*33*

*nights go on and we lie in our beds*
*overlooking the water*
*you're overlooking a lake*

**41**

*i'm overlooking the ocean*
*and you dream*
*about running down the city streets*
*from the darkness*
*but no one can hear you scream*

*you find yourself alone*
*in a perfect hell*
*and my heart is aching*
*because of what you feel*
*we are so connected*
*i feel what you feel when you feel it*
*i feel what you feel how you feel it*

*34a*

the PDFs i sent you
the journals, diaries of my life

the photos i sent you
still shots inhabiting a miracle of our own time

the videos i sent you
you remember the truth
in our eyes
when we were together

*34b*

my heart has been destroyed

*35*

*i want to be far away from the life i've been given*
*i want words to come to my mind*
*that will make the world understand*
*we are more than the colour of our skin*

*we are more than what our ancestors did*

*and the crimes we had nothing to do with*
*we do not extend the invitation*
*to equality*
*to be together*
*to live together*
*you threaten us with death*

*36*

i remember Harmonie,

i am still on this train
and she follows me forever
through life and death,
they are the same,
all a part of time,
all a part of eternity
and eternity is slowly moving
like the movement of the train
on the ground as we move from city to a new city
one i have never been in before
i walk the streets of Chicago
the worst part of town
i will find something to believe in
when i take all of the risks in the world
begging God to end it
be merciful to me
do to me what you did to her

you take my pain away
when you put me to sleep
you take my pain away
when i see her face
i know if i don't wake up
i will see it forever

*i do not see grace in the world*
*people all over are clamouring for change*
*but you don't hear us,*
*you don't know us*
*you've never seen what we look like*
*we hide beneath the shadows*
*we die and rise again*
*we haunt you for all eternity*
*you will notice us*
*but you won't know who we are*
*you won't know about the lives we've lived*
*because you've taken the grace from the world*
*if there was grace you would see us*
*if there was charity you would be set free*
*from the chains you don't notice around you*
*from the fetters clamping down on your hands*
*from now on the world will have no hope*
*you've died and made your choice*

*i am convinced*
*that there is hope*

*i am sure*
*you will find me*
*when you look for me*

*i am convinced*
*that there will be peace*

*i am sure*
*you will find me*
*when you dream of me*

*i am enthralled with the simple and beautiful*
*world*

*i am in love with the moments that pass*
*slowly*

                    *as the waters approach the shore*
*they soak my feet*
                    *as the storm begins to calm*
*i catch my breath*
                    *as the days begin to evaporate*
*i spend the rest with you*
                    *in the morning after the rain*
*we will both*

                    *see little miracles*

### 39

        with

        the loss of you i lost my hope

        with

        the setting of the sun on that day
        i never woke up happy again

        i lost my balance
        and fell headfirst into the concrete

### 40

*when i explore the world      i know*

*many of the faces i see*

*i will never see again*
*when i was soaring above everyone*
*and then my feet hit the ground*
*i had a revelation*
*that we have agency over our own world*

*but we don't believe it*

> *together we*
> *become more than the sum*
> *of who we are individually*
> *together we build our world*
> *and let the beauty of the world*
> *tell us who we are*
> *you show me the beauty of the world*

*and from then on when i look*
*at the beauty of the world*
*i always see you in it*

*you are full of what my dreams are full of*

the skyscrapers looming over the slums
              the torture that fills our lungs
when we remember
we almost made it out of poverty
we almost had a perfect life

i will hitch a ride on a train and sit in the boxcar
and write poems
all of them about the day
i lost you
and the day you lost your life

              the words you said
              are the words i will remember

"remember when you were young
and you thought that you could never die
and how the years crawl forward
and people will realize that they lost their innocence
when they chose
to degrade us for no reason

when my skin touches your

there is peace"

41

when i had a job,
i would spend hours at work
working as hard as possible
but nothing i did was good enough
now i am freezing at night
with no way to feed myself
no way to become someone more than who i am

42

with the music blaring from my speakers
we dance together
we're the only ones in the room
i don't want life to end
because there are so many things to love
about life,
the greatest of these is you

now i spend my days locked in a room
writing poems about the light
and also the darkness
where we don't know where we are
or where we are going

the fire from the volcanoes illuminates our future

i love the way you look in my eyes
and the way you smile wide

i miss the way you looked at me
when you were still alive

we run through the city
and are in love with the sights we see

and now everything i see makes me sad
because you are not here with me

your memory fades as the world disappears
and i fall asleep

voices inside my head    reminding me of my mistakes

forgetting the days of our youth
foolish dreams that we could ever be together
or that equality would be extended to us

each hour passes more slowly than the last,
when our rights are taken away from us,
when we have our home taken away from us
we will no longer feel invigorated
by the spirit of our youth
a conclave of people we've never met
decide our fate,
that we are not worth the payment for what we've been
working for

fire destroys our homes

the light fades underneath my bedroom door
in my youth
when i was holding you
now i have lost you
i found you and i held my hands to your face
but now i have lost you
i will always write the saddest lines
i will only write words that attempt
to unravel the twist in my own heart

with her i felt          invincible
without her i feel       invisible
with her                 i will always tell the truth
without her i am         living an eternal lie

with her there is peace   without her there is no religion
with her there can be no anguish
just love for the beautiful world

and together we would
be surrounded by the music inside us
saying "i'd give up forever to touch her"
saying "i met you at 17 and you mean the world to me"

all of the words now have become tears,

the only way to love is to trust you completely
and i don't care what happens next

### 43

you look at me and my eyes look different
        we don't talk like we used to
                your touch feels so distorted,
                        and i am totally to numb
                                to the feeling of your love

you say "Liefie i love the feeling of you,"
while i am numb to you
and i don't believe i'll be able to feel
anything touching me ever again
if i cannot feel you on my skin,
i will never feel you on my soul

### 44

*i love being held by you,*
*i love your hands on my face*
*i love how our skin melts together*
*i love how hard it is to let go of you*

*when you played that song on your cassette player*
*all i wanted to do was dance*
*all i could do was cry out, the sensation itself is to die for,*

49

*there is a feeling i have when i realize that*
*i will never be who i dreamed*
*but i'm with you and i can forget about*
*what i wanted my life to be before*

*we drink together and sit on the bonnet of your car,*
*you look so beautiful with*
*the pen in your hands,*
*knowing that you could express anything*
*your words could melt and reform the world*
*devastation and reconstruction*
*we destroy what we are to rebuild and rise again*
*the cycle of creation,*
*the CDs you sent me i listen to them every night*
*and dream that i am far away*

*i could spend the rest of my days*
*in countries i would never visit again*

*there is more to touch than skin touching skin*
*there is nothing more to our souls touching*
*each other, than that simple fact,*
*when my soul touches yours*
*there is no further need for any more spiritual expression*

*45*

each day we forget more and more
about our past
and as our lives shift from where they were
nothing ever stays the same,
there is music that will never be written
these songs will tell us the truth,
that is if songs ever had real power by themselves

the moonlight on my face

you said you would never leave
you will always be my only one

and i mean what i say
that even though the world is chaotic
and even though you have flaws i see right through them
i see something beautiful whenever i look at you

we built a home together
we built a world together
we made the memory eternal together

i hold you close deep in my arms
and all you will think about from then on
is mortality

how every vision we've ever seen
is always unreachable,
always intangible,
always phantasmal
always forgettable

*46*

*in our darkest days*
*the city we used to love*
*becomes the place where our nightmares take place*

*in our darkest hours*
*the vulnerability inside our souls*
*becomes so clear that we will never hide it again*

*there will be no saviour*
  *when we are crying out for help,*
  *blood dripping down our face,*
  *running through these empty streets*
  *where darkness grows with each passing second*

  *tragedy, we fall into you*
  *tragedy we disappear,*
  *we were so close to being free*
  *and now we are lost forever and ever.*

  *Amen.*

CD #2

.

*together we will have peace,*
*together we are all falling*
*through eternity*
*together we are all forgetting*
*about the days we were together*
*and didn't care what race we were when we were kids*
*programmed from early on,*
*to hate because of the colour of our skin*

*Liefie, you are my balance*
*you are the one i feel when*
*i am forgetting how to love,*
*how to become more than*
*who i am superficially*
*there is no superficial change*
*that would ever make me stop*
*loving you*

*Liefie, with you i am happy,*
*never going to leave you*
*falling into an ocean*
*where we will drown together*
*but i will never transcend this nation,*
*never be looked passed,*

i had a dream that you left me
because no one would hire me

and then i was on the street with no place to go
and then i went far away from here
and was never seen again,

*49*

*the simple moments with you*
*we are laughing together*
*i breathe in new life every day*
*together we sip on beer,*
*together we go explore the world*
*and sit by the lake*
*and inhale the air*
*and become one with it*
*really we could travel anywhere*
*we could be any two people we want to be*
*together*

*50*

i cried when i heard that song on the radio
because it told me to be in love with life
to take in every breath like it was my first
it taught me to love you and i fell in love with you
we drove in your car for miles and miles
there is something about songs that
we will never understand
there is truth in melody,
the days pass
and new songs are written
we will remember them all

*51*

*my happiness is overwhelming*
*i don't want to think about the future*
*my mind is on the here and now*
*if today could last forever,*
*i would always be happy*
*me and you existing in perfect concord*

## 52

*the world is peaceful*
*when the silent wind caresses my skin gently*
*like your touch and like a miracle*
*that has come to save your life*
*from certain disaster but*
*when you least expect it to happen*

## 53

when you left i felt like i would never
make a work of art again

now i try to paint something beautiful
and the picture is ugly to me

## 54

another night we spend together,
out looking at the stars
the most beauty that could ever exist
i found it all in you
how within the universe there is infinite possibility
infinite ways that i could love you
infinite things i could say

another night we spend apart
now i am alone in the forest
dreaming about you
i wish magic was real
i wish we were lost together
and that we will never go home

because the only home i need is your arms

breathing in the free air,
inebriating, liberating,
promising all things
fulfilling all things
including the fact that you will come back to me
that you will find me and take me far away with you
that you will be alive again
caught in your spell,
in love with the beautiful things,
in love with the beautiful trees,
in love with the beautiful world

i can feel you here,
i can feel your breath on my face as i reach down
to kiss you

*55*

*there are no voices of reason*
*in the middle of the mob*
*calling for our deaths*

*i will be the rational voice*
*in the darkness of so many errors*

*race is superficial*
*do not judge me because my skin is black or white*
*do not kill me because my skin is black or white*
*do not refuse to hire me because*
*my skin is black or white*
*do not stop loving me because my skin is black or white*
*do not judge me based on what my ancestors did*

*if all you care about*
  *is my race*
  *then you have lost your soul*

*one day i was walking toward the podium*
  *and then i was stabbed five times in the chest*
  *and then i was dead*
  *and then i was gone*
  *i knew that if this happened my voice would never echo*
  *through eternity*

  *i am reckless with my love,*
  *i feel as if there is no one i cannot be there for*
  *no one who is beyond saving*

*56*

the sounds of the world at night
the world smells different
the night has a distinctive smell
and i am at peace

i lost my Harmonie
i fell and tripped and learned
that every good thing
will always eventually be lost forever

*57*

she (Harmonie) is the beauty
that most people in the world rejected
that most people weren't ready for that helps
us break out of routine

the president of her country said

"we are not calling for the mass genocide of your entire
race....yet"

i said "fuck you,"

and then there was silence
and then there was violence inside my head

American reporters came here and interviewed him about
racial murders

everything he believed was wrong
based on myth and not reality
and in reality all of us are equal

my skin is so dark it shines
in the light but can't tell the difference
when we look in the illuminating light
Harmonie's skin is so beautiful,
i wouldn't care what color it is

different bright and dark and clear shades, make no
difference to me

*58*

*"we are not calling for mass genocide....yet"*

*i am calling for your resignation now*

*59*

when the spark of life is dying
i will still be believing in a better world

when the days are passing slowly
i will still be telling you how wrong you are
in telling me to despair

when i can no longer remember
the truth that gives me hope
i will fall into a cycle that
i cannot escape from


O poverty,
silence that happens when
the spark of life is gone
when we forgot how to love

*60*

walking through the streets of New York City,
i was excited to be in the world


walking through the empty streets of Chicago
i have lost all my joy


you were walking through the streets of Durban
with a message of hope in your heart
knowing that everything is possible
that there will be re-creation,
we will regain anything that is destroyed
we will build a world,
that we've always dreamed of
whatever is purged in flames
will eventually return to us


your hope is contagious,
it spreads like forest fire in the heat of summer
it spreads like the truth
that underlines our destinies


when
i am walking down the broken road
life takes me through
hope will be my guide
to light my steps
and lead me back home

61

i was forced to go to a mental ward for no good reason

and i began to miss the sunlight
and it melting into your face

and when i was finally free
i would spend hours
trying to type your number into my phone
but every time i tried to type it the app crashed
and i couldn't contact you

62

i had a dream that we were walking through the streets
together
and that a gun was pointed at you
and i knocked the weapon out of his hands

63

*i had a dream*
*that as the days went by*
*your touch felt colder and colder*
*until i couldn't feel you without feeling the seething cold*
*but i kept my body close to you anyway*
*because otherwise my soul would be cold*
*whenever i touch you my soul is warm*
*and at peace*

*64*

my poverty is overcoming me
but i don't mind


the sun sets and i wake up
and struggle to find some food,
struggle to leave this city
on my two feet


*65*


i like the way you move slowly and silently in the moonlight
the shadow of you across the bedroom floor
we step onto the balcony and look out at the city
where in the next five years i will walk across the same city
without you
i miss you the most when i am dreaming
i dream of you the most when i am wide awake
i wanted out of the machine of
a dull and dreary life,
everything i've found in you
the opposite of a
dull and dreary life


*66*


*i am walking alone through*
*the streets of Durban*


*i am thinking about the past*
*everything i've lost in you*
*eternity and peace,*
*i will show the nation what*
*the voices around me will never preach*

*67*

my faith is wearing thin
my nights are growing longer
when they grow longer
they grow colder
when i'm not with you


my love is fading away
my days are getting shorter
because i look forward each day
to being alone with my thoughts
losing hope of a better world
since the day they murdered you


*68*

*i am now in heaven*


*i am far away from you*


*you pray to me to beg God,*
*to change the motion of the world*
*but what you really want you never ask*
*you never ask for me to come back*
*without me, you say, the world is out of balance*
*falling over under its own weight,*

*69*

*i never want to leave you again.*

*70*

dark
empty
cold
at night
broken
freezing
shivering
memories fading of the past


i am coughing and the air is freezing
i am drowning in a dream
in which there is harmony in the world

*71*

**we would sit down together and create beautiful art**

**we always fell headfirst into every chaotic dream**

**we always wanted to show the world
how beautiful it is**

**but it kept telling us that it was ugly
inside and out**

we never gave into the world or believed a word it said
even when it looked uglier than a nightmare
we will never escape from
even when it became everything we revolted against
we never gave up on the world
we always daydreamed about it
we always knew the world would come
back to its true self
we always believed and hoped


*72*


winter in Paraguay, a day to forget about the past


spring in Paraguay, the world around opens up
and shows its true self


the future is fearful the future is trepidation
the past when it is gone is torture


*73*


poetry is what brings us together
the anthem of our lives


it is the music of the common man
the melody that changes the world
when everyone can speak its language


to see inside your heart
to know what is deeper within your soul


we will never run out of words


67

because we will always be trying
to undo what the world has become

*74*

my love for my own life went away
when the days started to pass slowly
when there was nothing to look forward to each day
when i realized that i had lost you
when i realized you were dead

grief never went away
when the days passed in the shadow of the dark clouds
when the clouds stayed where they were
for several years and didn't move at all
this began when i realized i had lost you
when i realized you were dead

i wish love could bring us together
i wish the charity inside me was enough
i wish emotions had a connection to the physical world
i wish i could create art again

*75*

*can you hear me in the darkness?*
*searching for your hand?*

## 76

*at night i am walking through this city once again,*
*trying to find my way back home*
*but i don't know where home is*
*i don't know where you have gone*
*your arms are my home*

## 77

*let the revolution begin,*
*let your joy be your norm of justice*
*let your peace be your reassurance of victory*
*let your love be your only weapon*

## 78

i was remembering Harmonie
and silently praying
and then i saw myself standing before the
National Assembly
thinking about death and decay
and speaking about atrocities
past present and future
i don't know how i got there so quickly
last second i was standing in front of the homeless shelter
about to leave
but we can travel great distances in a poem
without spending any money


the representative from The United States of America now
has the floor


i have come here to tell you a story
about one of your own

who was gunned down and knifed at the podium


you didn't listen to her
but i have seen her future,
in life or death your country will be transformed


too often
we drive a wedge between us and our humanity


we are not accountable for anything our ancestors have
done

      anyone who teaches this is in grave error and will
      lose their soul


dreaming of the video of Harmonie
being slaughtered by the street
like being eaten alive by mosquitoes slowly
we have lost touch with our humanity
i am not any race.  i am American
she was not any race.  she was South African
her blood ran red together with yours
and this blood has mingled with mine
our son was alive inside her
almost ready to be born
when he was slaughtered along with her
our son belongs to no nation
but the kingdom of heaven


blessed are the poor in spirit
for theirs is the kingdom of heaven
blessed are the merciful for


they will be shown mercy

bless those who hate you

remember to forgive
your past does not define you

i am dreaming of a world where
there is no poverty

where we give everything we have to others
where we do not waste any of our money on ourselves

we are not far from it
we can almost attain it
we can almost taste it

my parents were murdered when i was young
they were of African descent
my wife was murdered a few months ago.
she was of European descent




i walked outside
and was shot once in the head
and found myself in the hospital for five years

*79*

broken hearts spreading across
the world like a disease

some people break other's hearts for recreation

*80*

i lie alone on a hospital bed


my life will never be the same
i am happy with the life i have lived
and every work of art i have created
all i ever wanted was to make an imprint on the world
Harmonie, we made an imprint on the world together


i dream at night that you are with me with what is left of
my mind
i dream within a dream
i wake up and think i have really woken up
but then i wake up again
and you are really gone


*welcome home, my Liefie, here at the end,*
*we will be together forever*
*and forever never ends*


*the core of our souls was filled with hope*
*even though the world rejected us*


*and descended into chaos we will have peace together*
*that the world will never have*


*because life on earth was hell, a shadow of the things*
*that were coming*

the world without us


when we were together
i was bursting with passion


the nation without us


when we were separated
i was motionless


the province without us


when you stood there
with no way to balance yourself
you knew i had lost my life


the city without us


when you were gone
a week later i was devastated
and spiralled out of control
spent all my money and went to live on the street


OUR HOME without us
an empty bed,
during your last night on earth
you were not in my arms

the corpse of yesterday is devoured by animals
and never seen again
the bones dry up and lie there, sinking into the sand
killed by the disease of inequality,
destroyed by prejudice of those who never met you
who have never even seen you
who have never even heard your voice or name


euphoria of what could have been


we will write about the way
that world may have been
but we will never experience it
we will dream about it
but dreams were never experience
they always leave one wanting
we forget
 the present moment
we discover
what we are lacking in every human person
the only thing we lack is someone to care about
and to give our whole selves to

*82*


*the blood is still on your hands*
*put down your weapon*
*and beg for forgiveness*
*for everyone you have murdered*
*life isn't worth living, if you must kill another to*
*survive*

### 83

i sat in creative writing class dreaming
about words that would change your mind
but then realized it wasn't worth it,
your mind isn't worth changing
if i have to convince you of it

### 84

*so many beautiful things in the world*
*so many beautiful sounds*
*i hear birds and music*

*i am writing till i can no longer move my fingers*
*you will hear my voice*

### 85

*i want to do what is unexpected,*
*i want to be someone i thought i would never become*
*you are not defined by your past mistakes*
*in the new moment i think you could become anyone*
*i want to start a movement that is bigger than myself*

### 86

*imagine how sad the world would be*
*without good things to look forward to*
*believe me, many live this way*

*87*

**create something beautiful with me**

*88*

*we sat on the bench in the middle of the forest*
*talking about what we aspired to do in the future*
*and what we thought might happen*
*we ended up being wrong about almost everything*
*but we were right about what we felt*

*89*

*i am growing tired of wanting*
*and needing instead of thriving*

*90*

in a small town in Virginia i wait for you

and then get up and take your hand

in a big city in Hawaii we flee the state together
so that we can escape from volcanic eruptions
and create a new home together because we will never see
our old one again

we go to a club and dance slowly
we could really be anywhere in the world

## 91

broken glass on the floor
from the broken windows the rocks were thrown through
days when the fire from
the burning buildings has finally been extinguished

broken bottles of the wine
that we drank together
now somewhere we will never find
shattered across the floor

we were in your car driving somewhere
i can no longer recall where we went

## 92

the world is bright and then it gets darker

i am thinking about leaving and going somewhere
where i never will feel cold again
somewhere south of the equator

## 93

*i want to run far away from here*
*as fast as i possibly can*

*i want to be where i am in my dreams*
*with you on the couch fallen asleep*
*your hands stroking my head*

*you comforting me whenever i am in distress*
*and i will do the same for you*
*whenever you need me to*


*we'll share a front door together*
*we'll share our lives together*
*we'll love and raise our children*
*to love and re-create the world*
*fight for the world you love*
*believe that we can change*


*fight for peace*
*and live with joy like gasoline*


*overthrow your own heart*
*overthrow what is inside of you*
*a simple message will overcome the world*
*we've known it all along*
*we see what our future is*


*together forever*
*we are totally united*


*marching in the streets*
*not just in the streets but in every classroom*
*we will go back to the way it was when we*
*were children*
*our empty hearts can be filled with anything*
*the world looks brighter in the blinding sunlight*
*without it we are in the dark*


*i look out at the road that i am traveling on*
*it goes on forever to our destiny*
*believe me, it will be beautiful,*
*if you are brave enough to fall headfirst into it*

*the water will be warm and peaceful*
*and you will feel calm and fearless*
*as soon as you touch the water*

*one day we will be together*
*and we will never again not be together*

94

*sometimes i feel distraught*
*but i never feel alone*
*you are always here for me*
*whenever i am upset*

95

i was on the street and starving
but there was no place to go
no one to help us
or give us medical care

96

not very long ago,
i was happy
and it is amazing how life can change so quickly

the poets we will never hear
if we don't listen closely
poetry can come at times you don't expect it
it can be in the voices of
people you love
or people you walk by and do not help

*as long as i breathe,*
*i will be fighting*

*as long as i exist*
*there will be conflict*
*and we will never overcome it*
*but i will fight it because of what i believe*
*about eternity*
*and the nature of the end of all things*

today is the longest day of my life
anxiety about what will happen next
i keep my eyes glued to the television

*never forget the hope within your own soul*
*there is healing when you realize*
*that it doesn't matter how hurt you become*
*when you fight for what is true*

*100*

i believe in things i have never seen
i long for days i will never live through
i long for the moment when we are together
even in the dark,

*101*

*forgiveness which we have forgotten*
*which we no longer comprehend*
*everyone needs it*
*and is in turmoil when it is gone*

*102*

today we are together
listening to the same songs
and you don't believe the same things i do
but it brings us together in peace

*103*

*my phone is about to die*
*and i am in the middle of the city*
*and i feel i will be lost forever*

*i fall asleep in the city*
*and never leave*
*and dream that one day i will be far from it*

*i run away to another city*
*and i meet strangers*

and greet each one on the street
our revolution starts here
with the seasons my mood always changes
with the passing days
i slowly see the changes in the world come into effect


i dream that the world is changing quickly
at the same rate every second and faster than it ever has
a revolution each day
little changes affect the world around us
and then the world itself


whenever i come to one city
i want to move to another
i can never feel settled
i am always uneasy
i have always felt the need to move
and be somewhere other than where i am
be somewhere or anywhere with you


i am staring at the sky
gazing at the stars

*104*

our freedom of speech
nights spent relaxing and talking with you
the ability to search for the truth
and to find it
the way you hold me close
the days we can spend at peace
the morning before the rain
the morning of the rain
the morning after the rain
the morning when the skies are clear
the morning when the skies are dark
the night when we can see the stars clearly
the night when the stars are covered by clouds
the days when we dance together
the nights when we drink together
the moment when you told me you loved me
for the first of countless times
the moment when i come home
after spending an entire day at work
the days we spend together
exploring every part of the world that we can
the way you smile at me
the way you laugh at what i say
the closeness i feel from you
the warmth i feel from you
the light you shined onto my life
that drove away the darkness
how you make me feel fulfilled
how no day will pass again
without me being happy
(i have everything i've ever needed)
the American standard
that flies in every city of my country
the South African standard that flies above yours
and represents the hopes of your people
the days when we stand in church

and make a promise to God before the altar
how we have not given into despair
how with you there is always something
like truth of the hope of our future
despite the despair of the here and now
the truth i find in the scriptures
the quietness of when i am alone in my room
the peace i am justified through
when you are here with me
the days when i know you will be with me again
(i always count them down)
the kisses on my face that you give me
(and the ones you receive from me)
the revolution we started together
which will burn down and rebuild our nations
the books i read about lands far away
that never existed
and inspire me to become something more than i can ever
possibly become
the songs that we listened to together
that make us feel like conquering the world
and weathering through the storm of life
the pictures on the wall that remind me of the past
the mirror i see you in
that reminds me of our future
together
the anthem of our lives
that will be heard righteously and justly
in the story of our lives together
the CDs i hand out to people in Chicago and Durban
showing the Unity we will have together
and will never be able to escape from
(yes, our destinies are fixed and set
there is absolutely nothing we can do to escape from it)
the strangers i meet on the street
and the words they say afterwards about the poverty
they are dealing with
the years that i know will go by with us together
the family we will raise

the front door we will share
a kiss in the rain
a dance in the rain
the celebration we had when
we knew we might lose everything
but if we lose our lives we will find them
how i feel like i am complete and lacking nothing now, with
faith hope and charity
how you only need to imagine and act on the world you
want and then it is here with us
how we fight against regimes that want to take our homes
it is a privilege to fight and be alongside, my Harmonie,
how at night you are here to comfort me
even when you are
eight thousand miles away the sky
the boundless and beautiful world
the trees around us that remind us
when we were lost in the woods
and believed that magic was real
and knew we could travel from
one corner of the world to the other
you are not ethereal, you are not a ghost,
you are as real as you possibly could be
you are someone who loves being held
you are always kind
and never jealous
never pompous or rude
you never take offense
how your heart is big enough not only to hold me
but to hold the entire world
the tv light when have both fallen asleep at night
how you are so close and when you are far away
i know i will see you again tomorrow
the stories i read about heroism
and the virtues that we can easily have
it is better to be virtuous than to lead a comfortable life
the story that will be read about our lives,
the way music makes me feel
(it's always the way i feel with you)

the way we celebrate the lives we have together
through expression and through the ecstatic joy we feel
how we could be anywhere in the world right now
(it is truly possible)
how you are in love with the beautiful world
the days we spent together when we were young
we will never settle down
always will be in motion together
how my joy is so obvious in my life
how it underlines every word i say
and everything that i do
i love when you are here in the darkness
when everyone else is gone
(we will share this message with the world
it is always necessary to be there for those in need)
i love when you are here listening
when no one else is listening
and because of this i will no longer desire
anyone else to listen
when you and i are gathered
God is here
how we are together for Thanksgiving
even when we are the only ones there
and i will be reading this long list to you
how i cried when you told me how much you loved me
and everything you love about me
how i can share the love you gave me
with the rest of the world
and i believe it will not only save my world
but all worlds
if you are here in the sunlight
i know this light illuminates our scars and makes
them very beautiful
i love how i can never stop saying i love you
and how you want to spend the rest of your life with me
how i never want to think about the future
except when i think about you and me
how redemption finds us all and brings us together
like we share the same DNA

and become part of the same person
i love the way my friends were here for me
to help me spread my art
how you caught me when i fell
and how i would do the same for you
(we all need to be resurrected but first we need to die)
how the world is so colorful,
you taught me how to see things clearly with my own eyes
i am now strong enough to stand my own ground
and to support my family
i am grateful for you and your face on my hands
as we come inside
the night of the rain
and how on the day of the storm
i was able to get home safely
and will never be afraid of the wind
and the rain again
how we ran through the city together
and realized
there are so many new things to experience
so many new skills to learn
but step by step we will fight
to become the people we want to be
the records we play during the evening
and then fall asleep
and when i sleep i have dreams within a dream
and when i wake up it gets happier and happier
and i wake up wondering where i am
but i am happy to be with you
how we lurch out against the injustice
poisoning the world
threatening to drown us in its cold embrace
how together we can fight for liberty
and how no one can ever shut my mouth
or force me to put down my brush or pen
how the words that are strongest within my heart are
love poems
how the days that pass the quickest
are the ones when i'm with you

i can feel your warmth when you are gone
you are never satisfied with the world
you are fighting for the one you love
the days we spend watching movies
some scary, some happy
but through all of them you are here with me
how our worlds have changed overnight
the snow
september in the rain
the days i spent inside painting
(i painted a portrait of you
and i feel it encapsulated who you are)
how we are growing closer to the beauty
of the world each day
the words you say to me now
the words you say to me tomorrow
the words you said to me when we first met
how when are stranded in the city
i am still here with you and you haven't let go of me
the summer heat we feel as we walk through the forest
the fall breeze that we feel as we walk through the town
the freezing cold as we walk through the city
the joy i felt when i met your family for the first time
we will never forget the time
when we first met
the time i gave you a piece of my heart
forever
forever is so long and incomprehensible
at some point you will forget some of the things you love
as long as i exist i will never forget about you
the trip we took to Norway
the beautiful fjords we saw
how the ship broke the water creating ripples and waves
and the relief we feel knowing that we have enough to eat
you embrace the beautiful things in the world
there is always more to say
there is always more to write about
there are always more pictures to paint
there is always more to love

always more to show about the world
always time to think about the present moment
i am grateful that the world is willing to change
i am grateful for all of these things

## 105

*what is the reason for pain?*

*ans.*
*so that you can hold onto me while you are going through it*

*why is there so much tension in the world?*
*ans.*
*there is tension so that we can recognize the beauty when it is gone,*
*when there is harmony and peace*

*without the peace in our lives we have nothing*

i want to create beautiful poems
that let you know exactly what i am feeling


so that we can
be who we always wanted to become


if you ever need someone to guide you
through the storm
i will be here
if you ever need someone to show you the beauty
after the storm
i will be here
you breathe the generous air
you take in every moment like it will be your first
and your very last
you take in every feeling like you will never feel
anything again


you look at pictures of all the places you can travel to


and you know you may never go to any of those places


i spent my days playing video games
but dreaming about other worlds


i wish i could find myself away from here


i need to fly away


i need to become more than i can imagine

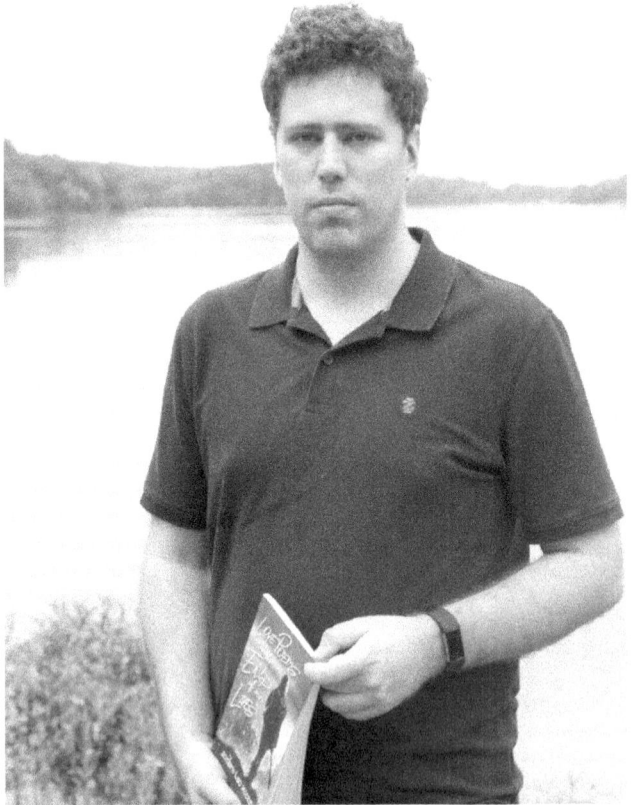

Joseph Leo Hickey lives in VA. He is the author of four other poetry books, including *Baptism of Apathy*, *Unity* and *Love Poems at the End of Our Lives*. He is a double graduate of George Mason University and is currently 26 years old.

YouTube: allthestarsaredead

freedominspring12@gmail.com

www.ingramcontent.com/pod-product-compliance
Lightning Source LLC
LaVergne TN
LVHW051704080426
835511LV00017B/2713